Hogarths Epic Poem

Terry J Powell

AuthorHouse™ UK
1663 Liberty Drive
Bloomington, IN 47403 USA
www.authorhouse.co.uk
UK TFN: 0800 0148641 (Toll Free inside the UK)
UK Local: 02036 956322 (+44 20 3695 6322 from outside the UK)

Because of the dynamic nature of the Internet, any web addresses or links contained in this book may have changed
since publication and may no longer be valid. The views expressed in this work are solely those of the author and do not
necessarily reflect the views of the publisher, and the publisher hereby disclaims any responsibility for them.

Any people depicted in stock imagery provided by Getty Images are models,
and such images are being used for illustrative purposes only.
Certain stock imagery © Getty Images.

This book is printed on acid-free paper.

ISBN: 978-1-6655-8711-2 (sc)
ISBN: 978-1-6655-8710-5 (e)

Print information available on the last page.

Published by AuthorHouse 03/08/2021

authorHOUSE®

Hogarths Epic Poem

. . . .

The old Warlock stood there in his place.

Calling the old gods and forces of nature to his face

I command you to appear

I stand protected and have no fear

HOGARTH does command

To help us mortals here at hand

. . . .

Rise up, rise up, I call on you as I have need

Assist me with my mystical deed

I command you by all the gods that's I known

Appear before me spirit of GOAN

For I have need of your services, from your grave

I beckon you, my slave

....

Wind, Storm, Torrent came

Howling voices in moaning pain

*HOGARTHS greying hair and beard tossed in winds
that blew*

Ghouls in a circle, Spirits flew

With tempest all around

The warlock stood his ground

Once again I shout GOAN I command thee to come

You are in my power till my deed is done

. . . .

From darkest gates of hell

Spawned a foul and ghastly smell

A dark silhouette writhing against his will

Screaming a deathly howl in a deafening shrill

I HOGARTH command you not to resist

You are in my power I insist

As the creature rose on earth to full height

His massive form swamped the night

....

A creature with leather blue grey skin

Like a crocodile covering with horns set in

Tall and hunched

Face taught, twisted, and slightly bunched

Deepest eyes or glowing yellow red

Thick set brow and malformed head

Protruding teeth yellowed with age

Thick lower lip taught with rage

....

GOAN roared "Who has summoned my here on this night from where I dwell?"

Booming voice that shook the depths of hell

I HOGARTH warlock of the place of When lock, I have called thee

I have the power over you to do my bidding for me

For You GOAN have a contract with me to fore fill

The demon spoke "Hogarth I am at your will"

What is this quest you will have me do?

Name this deed I do for you

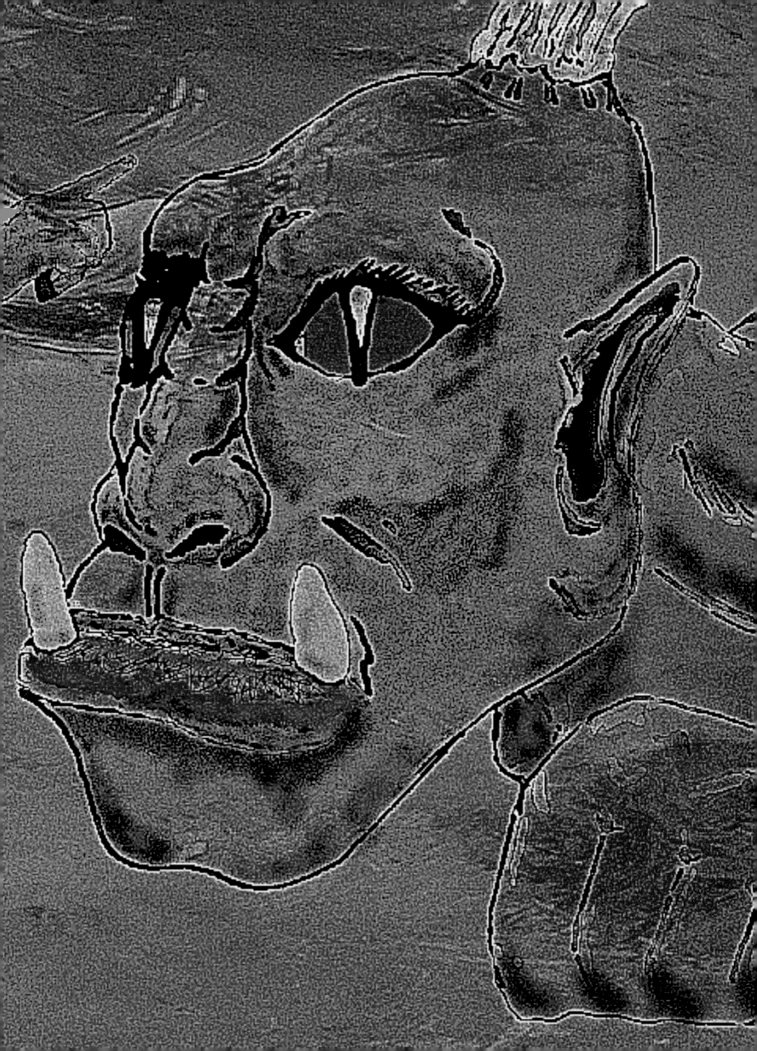

···············

I have an enemy that's cast on me his hex

Unto me, he has angered and made me vex

For this I seek revenge

I will not stop until avenged

Go seek him out and take his soul

This your reward when the deed is whole

For myself I take his powers to be mine

Those skills and property I can combine

. . . .

His name is DYTHON in the vale of dean

He's cruel, ruthless, and branded mean

Go GOAN bring him to me here in this place

So I can see the terror on his face

Goan roared writhing, twisting with pleasure and pain

HOGARTH waited for them to return again

·········

Time passed throughout the night when GOAN returned

Dumped down a sack, inside screams and pleading was heard

Goan picked up the sack and shook it about

DYTHON rolled out of the sack unto the ground and out

Mercy, mercy, he did plead

Cuts and bruises his wounds did bleed

……..

Goan Picked Dython up by his hands

Struggling foe went limp, helpless as he hangs

………

I take your powers DYTHON for my own

All your knowledge, properties, and your home

Spell now cast and all goods received

DYTHON now stripped and cruelly relieved

....

GOAN takes the poor wretch in to the gapping ground

HOGARTH listening to the screaming sound

Closed earth, now deed was done

Warlock HOGARTH victoriously won

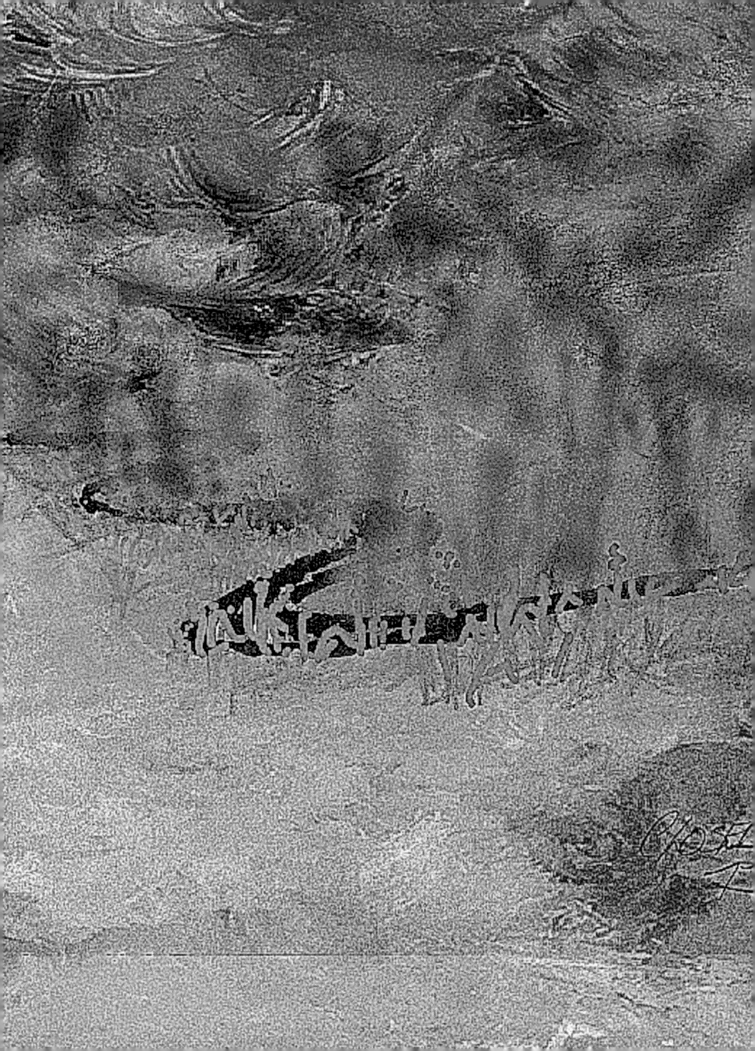

The End

Printed in the United States
by Baker & Taylor Publisher Services